THIN PLACES EVERYWHERE

The 12 Days of Christmas
with Celtic Christianity

BRUCE G. EPPERLY

THIN PLACES EVERYWHERE

The 12 Days of Christmas with Celtic Christianity

Copyright © Bruce Epperly, 2019.

Anamchara Books
Vestal, New York 13850
www.AnamcharaBooks.com

IngramSpark 2020 paperback ISBN: 978-1-62524-792-6

Scripture quotations are taken from the New Revised Standard Version Bible, copyright © 1989 National Council of the Churches of Christ in the United States of America. Used by permission. All rights reserved worldwide.

Illustrations by Aleksandr Velichko (Dreamstime.com).

Cover and page design by Micaela Grace.

CONTENTS

1. **A Celtic Christmas**	**9**
2. **Original Wholeness**	**19**
3. **Thin Places Everywhere**	**25**
4. **Holy Adventures**	**31**

THE 12 DAYS OF CHRISTMAS
Days of Incarnation and Adventure

5. **The Eve of Adventure: Christmas Eve** December 24	**43**
6. **The First Day of Christmas: Christmas Day** December 25	**49**
7. **The Second Day of Christmas** December 26	**55**
8. **The Third Day of Christmas** December 27	**61**

9. **The Fourth Day of Christmas**	
December 28	**69**
10. **The Fifth Day of Christmas**	
December 29	**75**
11. **The Sixth Day of Christmas**	
December 30	**81**
12. **The Seventh Day of Christmas**	
December 31	**87**
13. **The Eighth Day of Christmas**	
January 1	**93**
14. **The Ninth Day of Christmas**	
January 2	**99**
15. **The Tenth Day of Christmas**	
January 3	**105**
16. **The Eleventh Day of Christmas**	
January 4	**111**

17. **The Twelfth Day of Christmas**
    January 5   **117**

18. **The Adventure Continues:**
    The Feast of Epiphany
    January 6   **125**

Sources   **133**

.1.
A CELTIC CHRISTMAS

Joy to the world,
the Lord is come;
Let earth receive
her king.
Let every heart
prepare him
room,
And heaven and
nature sing,
And heaven
and nature sing,
And heaven and heaven
and nature sing.

(Isaac Watts)

Christmas is the shortest season of the Christian year, and in most households it's over almost as soon as it's begun. After ramping up for Christmas from Halloween through November and December, everything seems to halt after the presents are unwrapped, dinner served, and the decorations put away. We get on with life, despite the business and school lull between Christmas Eve and New Year's Day. Still, there is something in our spirits that longs for the season to continue into the New Year. We want to hold on to the warm-heartedness and generosity, the innocence and joy.

Christmas is the season of Incarnation, of the child in the manger, starry skies, shepherds, magi, and a migrant family. In the distance, we hear the singing of angels and aspire to embody the better angels of our nature in our daily lives and national priorities. The child in us awakens, reminding us that despite our sophisticated adult tastes, there really is a Santa Claus, and we can sojourn to Hogwarts on Track 9¾. A closet can be the portal to Narnia, and Madeleine L'Engle's Thinking Rock invites us to "tesser" across the universe. We are standing on holy ground, with millions and millions of angels all around.

Beyond the commercialism of Christmas is a deeper reality. The season is chockful of Divinity, wonder, and mysticism, just below the surface of shopping days and mad spending. We want more out of life than packages under the tree or the newest cyber toy. We yearn for daily doses of Divinity to brighten the dark days of winter and illuminate our personal and planetary pathways. We are saved, as Howard Thurman avers, when we attend to the singing of angels. Christmas is not just a long season of shopping followed by one day of partying; it is twelve days of adventure that beckon us to a lifetime of incarnational living.

As a pastor, I celebrate the days of Christmas, lighting candles on Christmas Eve, reading the sacred stories while the family sleeps on Christmas morning, and charting the path of the magi as I walk on Cape Cod beaches early on Boxing Day (December 26). For me, the days that follow have become occasions of awe and wonder, in which life pauses and I take stock of my calling as God's companion in healing the Earth. I ponder what it means to birth the Christ Child in my time and place.

For the past few years, during the Christmas season, I have focused my attention on a particular spiritual guide to keep me on the Christmas pathway. I have lived with the challenges of African American mystic Howard Thurman, who discovered the Incarnation among dispossessed persons like Mary and Joseph; Thurman invited me to find Jesus at the soup kitchen and on the borderlands of the United States. The following year, I journeyed across the universe with Madeleine L'Engle, learning to "tesser"—leap from one dimension to the other—and "kythe" my empathetic connectedness with all Creation. This year, my spirit was drawn to Celtic Christianity and its spirit of adventure, whether on the high seas, rocky coastlines, or craggy hilltops.

I wanted to pursue my own adventures with Christ as my companion on the familiar, yet surprising thoroughfares, of my own daily life. I discovered that embracing the Celtic Christian tradition illumined my faith and helped me chart a path of faithful adventure amid the threats and challenges of my own time. It gave me a space where I could join the chorus that "heaven and nature sing."

Celtic Christianity has enjoyed a revival over the last fifty years. The pilgrim spirit of the Celts and their affirmation of God's presence in the non-human world has inspired seekers within and beyond the Christian family. The "Christ of the Celts," described by Phillip Newell, takes us beyond any particular tradition to experience "God in all things and all things in God." We need this spirit as we face the apparently insolvable realities of global climate change, institutional hard-heartedness toward pilgrims caravanning from other lands, and the growing rifts over politics and lifestyle. We need to find a way, in the spirit of the Celtic Christians' hospitality to the Druidic tradition, to embrace the wisdom of Earth-based religions and the growing number of self-described "spiritual but not religious" persons—and to experience the Word and Wisdom of God in its varied and surprising disguises. In that spirit, I invite you to share in a Celtic Christmas Adventure for the season's twelve days, plus Christmas Eve and the Feast of Epiphany. Join me on a voyage with Brendan, Columba, Brigid, and Patrick over the high seas of spiritual adventure to find the Incarnational spot God intends for you.

Our guides to spiritual adventure, the Celtic Christian wise women and men, are a varied lot. In fact, the word "Celt" itself is vague and hard to pin down. But there is a virtue in vagueness. The God we claim to fully know or the person we think we've figured out completely is not the Living God or the embodied person we encounter. Still, amid the mists of Iona and the busyness of our hometown, we can discern the contours of the Celtic Christian landscape.

Today, Celtic Christianity is primarily identified with Ireland, Scotland, and parts of England. But, as Carl McColman asserts, these Celts "represent a tiny remnant of what was once a mighty culture, thundering across the continent in ancient times."[1] At their height, the Celtic people called much of Europe their home, and it is quite possible that Paul's ministry at Galatia—and the letter he wrote to the Galatians—was aimed at ancestors of today's Celtic Christians.

The meaning of the word "Celt" is itself somewhat vague. It may refer to "stranger" or "pilgrim." It may also refer to "high-spirited" or "elevated." The ancient Celts were storytellers, bards, poets, wizards, and warriors. They were peregrines and pilgrims, who loved not only to share tales of high adventure but also go on adventures into unknown lands. In the words of author and theologian Nelle Morton, the Celts believed that "the journey is home." From them we can learn that whether we are on the high seas or a woodland path, or even in the quiet of our study, the fullest life involves blending novelty and familiarity, movement and rest, creativity and tradition.

There is a tendency for us to romanticize the Celts, to see them through the hazy green mist of idealism rather than from the perspective of historical accuracy. Other authors have addressed this issue; my goal in this book is to garner what we can learn from the Celtic story, both historical and romanticized, and discover what practical and pragmatic use we can find for this story in our own twenty-first-century lives. And so, if we look at the central core of Celtic Christian spirituality, we find that it emerges from the interplay of three interdependent theological and spiritual movements, woven together by the gospel affirmation that "the true light, which enlightens everyone, was coming into the world" (John 1:9).

First, God comes to us through many voices and rituals, including the Earth-based or Pagan religions. The Celtic followers of Jesus experienced the Holy in the Son of God and also the heavenly sun of Pagan ritual. God is found in Druidic holy places—oak groves, wells, and crags—and in the passionate wisdom of bards and shamans. These Druidic thin places gave birth to Christian holy places and holy people. Christian incarnational theology found new expressions in dialogue with the deep earthiness of Druidic religion. There was a profound spiritual kinship between indigenous Celtic Paganism and its delight in the senses and the Earth-affirming spirituality of Jesus, for whom sparrows, grasses, mustard seeds, and children mediated God's realm to humankind. God is as surely present in the wisdom of the Druids as in the insights of the Hebraic and Greek peoples. In speaking of the indigenous spirituality of his time, Columba asserted, "Christ is my Druid."

Second, Celtic Christianity was profoundly influenced by the monastic spirit and often quirky Zen-like wisdom of the Desert Mothers and Fathers. Faith becomes passionate and fiery when lived out in monastic communities, grounded in the wisdom of the heavens but pointed toward the beauty of the Earth. Celtic Christians embraced the monastery within as they sailed high seas or hiked woodland trails.

Finally, Celtic Christianity followed the path of Pelagius in contrast to the way of Augustine. The fourth-century Celtic theologian has been derided as a heretic, but he plumbed the depths of scripture and tradition, where he discovered the deeper meaning of the Incarnation: God truly loves the world of the flesh. The world is to be embraced, not scorned. The body is an echo of the soul and not a prison house. God's pronouncement of the goodness of the universe and humankind describes our deepest nature. In a letter to a friend, Pelagius advised:

> Look at the animals roaming in the forest: God's spirit dwells within them. Look at the birds flying across the sky: God's spirit dwells within them. Look at the tiny insects crawling in the grass: God's spirit dwells within them. There is no creature on earth in whom God's spirit is absent. . . . God's spirit is present in all plants as well. The presence of God in all things makes them beautiful and if you look with God's eyes, nothing on earth is ugly.[2]

Pelagius believed that evil emerges from relationships and cultural values, but it is not original to human nature. He taught that women are vessels of revelation rather than occasions of sin. The glory of God, as second-century Christian spiritual guide Irenaeus affirmed, is a fully alive, fully embodied human.

Celtic spirituality lives on and invites us to a perpetual Christmas in its counsel to love God in the world of the flesh and delight in the beauties of nature. Following these Celtic adventurers enables us to embrace the spirit of Christmas—of God's incarnational love—with every new day, and sing "joy to the world" as each new "morning has broken."

.2.
ORIGINAL WHOLENESS

This little light of mine,
I'm gonna let it shine,
This little light of mine,
I'm gonna let it shine. . . .
Everywhere I go, I'm gonna let it shine,
Let it shine, let it shine, let it shine.

(Harry Dixon Loes)

As a pastor, I often find myself in unexpected conversations at wedding receptions. While I feel at home sitting with sinners and happy pagans, I am typically seated with the most "religious" relatives and attendees, and I often find myself embroiled in an unprovoked theological discussion in which I am called upon either to defend the sins of Christianity or respond to questions about my own orthodoxy as a Christian theologian and minister.

Sometimes, at a wedding rehearsal, even Calvin, Augustine, and Pelagius get in the mix. When our son was a toddler, my wife and I were seated next to the parents of another young child, the daughter of one of my wife's relatives. As the two children played, the father engaged me in a conversation. Knowing I was a pastor, he asserted, "You know my child is selfish and self-centered. That's human nature. She can't do anything about it. We are sinners by nature, even as toddlers. Born into sin, we're lost unless God saves us through the blood of Jesus."

I hesitated, knowing that whatever I said would be challenged. Finally, I responded with a degree of levity, "Well, your daughter may be a sinner, but my son isn't!" Thankfully, that ended our brief conversation on original sin, predestination, and human nature. I could now get back to my cocktail and hors d'oeuvres.

This fairly trivial conversation has its roots in one of the great tragedies of Christian history: the excommunication of the fourth-century Celtic theologian Pelagius as a result of the political intrigues of Augustine of Hippo. The opposing dinner-table comments reflected the contrast of Augustinian (Roman) and Pelagian (Celtic) theology.

Augustine saw human beings, including young children, as mortally infected by original sin. On our own, he taught, we can do nothing to save ourselves, and so we must depend wholly on the grace of God. Nature—whether the non-human world or human nature—is essentially corrupted by the sin of Adam and Eve and cannot be redeemed apart from God's unilateral redemptive activity through the Cross of Christ. Original sin, universally transmitted through the processes of procreation, characterizes our deepest nature. Like the toddler as described by her father, there is nothing "good" about us apart from Divine intervention. In fact, Augustine believed sin so defiled the human character that apart from baptism, people who died in infancy were condemned to a "twilight zone" known as limbo.

In relationship to God, according to Augustine's thinking, we are passive recipients of grace, and any agency or partnership on our part verges on ingratitude and infidelity. Augustine saw the character of God's grace toward humanity as all or nothing. Any human partnership with God, Augustine believed, denied the efficacy of grace, placing our salvation in our hands and not God's. To Augustine, God was a demanding Ruler, who gives but never receives from the created world and who is insulted by any spiritual initiative on the part of "His" subjects.

In contrast, Pelagius affirmed the original goodness of humankind. He taught that every child is created in God's image and is essentially good; every newborn child reflects God's creative wisdom. Building on this theology, the ninth-century Celtic theologian John Scotus Eriugena asserted, "Every visible and invisible creature can be called a theophany."[3] Pelagius recognized that sin is a real and tragic distortion of our deepest nature that obstructs our relationship with God, but he also knew that sin cannot destroy the original wholeness of humankind. Created and proclaimed good by our Creator, God's image is more durable than any sin we might commit. A person's behavior may change and be sinful, but the individual's inherent nature has not changed. Despite our imperfection, God continues to act providentially through Nature, scripture, experience, and ritual to restore and redeem what has been tarnished. Whereas Augustine saw humans as powerless before an all-powerful Divine Potentate who acts unilaterally for our salvation, Pelagius believed salvation involved a Divine-human synergy in which God's call elicits our faithful responses. Our agency and creativity give glory to God and further God's vision of wholeness and health—what the Bible calls *Shalom*.

Long before the Protestant theologian John Wesley, Pelagius affirmed God's prior or prevenient grace, but he equally affirmed God's intimate and empowering relationship with all Creation. Pelagius believed that both Nature and grace are gifts of God. Salvation occurs naturally, in the world in which we live, through God's graceful providence, rather than supernaturally from outside the natural processes that nurture and sustain us. God acts within the world of Nature, taught Pelagius, and within our own humanity to draw us toward wholeness. The "good of Nature and the good of grace" reflect God's omnipresent quest for Shalom.[4]

Shaped by Pelagian theology, Celtic spiritual guides saw God's light shining in every newborn's face. From this perspective, the light that shone in the Bethlehem stable enlightens every human child and shines more brightly as we grow in wisdom and stature. We are loved because of who we are as God's beautiful and beloved children, not in spite of our imperfection and fallibility.

Following the footsteps of the Holy Child of Bethlehem, we discover that the glory of God is a fully alive human being, embodying the Christ-like possibilities unique to every life. Spiritual practices and acts of kindness awaken us to the light of God within us—the Divine presence that enlightens everyone—so that we can let our light shine, giving God glory and bringing forth the glory of God in all Creation. When we let our light shine, the light of God bursts forth, illuminating our lives and healing the world.

.3.
THIN PLACES EVERYWHERE

Oh, little town of
Bethlehem how
still we see
thee lie
Above thy
deep and
dreamless sleep
the silent
stars go by
Yet in thy dark
streets shineth the everlasting light
The hopes and fears of all the years
are met in thee tonight.

(Phillip Brooks)

There are places, persons, and periods that define our lives and human history. On Christmas Day (and the exact date of Christmas is unimportant), the hopes and fears of humankind were gathered in the dream of planetary healing. A vortex of creative transformation filled the humble manger, transforming it to the *axis mundi*, the center around which all Creation revolves. In that stable, Heaven and Earth joined, humanity became transparent to Divinity, and all Creation sang; in Madeleine L'Engle's joyful language, the neutrino and unicorn danced. In that incarnational moment, a new energy emerged that would change history forever, the wise energy hidden and ready to be born in the Big Bang, the fourteen-billion-year universe journey, and the starts and stops of the human adventure. God's vision of beauty and wholeness was enfleshed in a "wee bairn" (as my Scots Highlander ancestors would say).

Celtic Christians and their Druid spiritual parents described such holy places as thin places. Groves of trees, rock formations, islands, wells, and springs were set apart as portals to Divinity, places where persons were transformed by holiness and the Holy One revealed deep wisdom and healing. The Druids believed in spots "where mortals could communicate with the denizens of Tir na n-Og, the spirit world."5 Places like Lindisfarne and Iona stand out among Celtic Christians as holy islands and places of pilgrimage. Other places, the Tor of Glastonbury, Stonehenge, Taos, Findhorn, Mecca, Jerusalem, the Bodhi Tree, and the Ganges River channel infinite Divinity to finite humanity. Pilgrims journey to such holy places in search of enlightenment, healing, and creative transformation. Grounded in Divinity—sand, soil, and sea—they discover their deepest identities as God's beloved children, called to a life of adventure and healing.

I recall one such thin place in the course of my own spiritual journey. During a teaching stint at Ghost Ranch, New Mexico, I experienced Divine revelation radiating from a hoodoo or chimney rock at the edge of the conference center. This Ebenezer, jutting heavenward in the wilderness, drew me toward it every morning. Though I believe God is equally present in earth and sky, the chimney rock awakened something deep in me. I felt the presence of the ancients who saw Divinity in mountaintops and rock formations. First-American shamans became my contemporaries as I recognized the holiness that surrounded and upheld me with each step.

God is present everywhere and in all things, and yet God may choose to be present more fully in certain places than others. We can't explain these intense reflections of Divine energy and wisdom, but we know from our own experience that not all moments of our lives are homogenous. I remember the first time, now over forty years ago, that my wife, looking up at me as we walked down the steps of her apartment house, whispered, "*Je t'aime*," "I love you," and a new possibility emerged, one that I have reaffirmed each day since that moment. Perhaps you discovered a deeper sense of God's presence at the birth of a child, the death of a spouse or parent, or transfixed by a starry, starry night. With nothing but a stone for a pillow, Jacob dreamed of a ladder of angels, ascending to the heavens and descending back to earth. There are thin places everywhere.

A conversation among rabbis centered around Moses' encounter with a burning bush. "Why was the bush burning, but not consumed?" the rabbis queried. They argued the point until one rabbi stopped discussion with the words, "It was burned but not consumed so that one day as he walked by Moses would finally notice it!" Thin places call us to attention; they make us notice the spiritual reality that is always and everywhere already present.

Thin places also give birth to "thin"—or transparent—persons, spiritual friends whose presence transforms our lives. The Celtic tradition describes the life-changing reality of soul friendship by the term Anam Cara (or *anamchara*)—someone with whom you share a soul. In such unique friendships, another person becomes the mirror of Divinity for you. You experience your own inner light and the holy light of another that goes beyond you to enlighten the world. Our Anam Cara awakens us to a spiritual reality that is more than we could ask or imagine, in which ordinary encounters and landscapes become charged with God's grandeur and we see our deepest selves, perhaps for the first time. Celtic Christians believed that Jesus was the ultimate Anam Cara, the friend of every soul, intimately encountering each of us as if there is only one of us and calling forth the light within, giving us courage to shine like stars in the universe. In encountering Christ, we discover our own inner Christ, the unique Divine vocation that is ours alone, blessing us and blessing the world.

Thin places also open us to "thin" times. Theologians speak of the contrast between *Kairos* (spiritual time) and *Chronos* (clock time) as representative of holy moments that emerge to change the landscape of our lives and the planet. At the right time, the Kairos moment, a child is born in Bethlehem. At the appropriate time, a mentor comes into our lives or we're ready to commit ourselves to a person or spiritual path. In the wondrous synchronicity of life, we can experience the gentle providence of God, working within all things, even negative experiences, to bring forth truth, goodness, and beauty. In God's gentle providence, certain moments reveal our calling, the calling of our congregation, and the calling of humankind.

We cannot magically conjure up such transparent moments and locales. We can however attend to the holy moment and then cultivate spiritual practices to welcome such theophanies, revealings of God, when they present themselves to us. In every millisecond and every meeting, Divinity calls, alerting us to the holiness of the moment in which we find ourselves. There are ladders of angels everywhere and burning bushes dot every pathway when the doors of perception, as William Blake wrote, are cleansed and we see all Creation as it is—*infinite*!

So, in a humble stable, the light of God shone and the domestic gave way to Divinity and the ordinary to revelation. In that and every holy moment, we can exclaim, "The hopes and fears of all the years are met in thee tonight."

.4.
HOLY ADVENTURES

Go, tell it one the mountain,
Over the hills and everywhere,
Go, tell it on the mountain
That Jesus Christ is born.

(African American spiritual)

The Celts were adventurous people. According to legend, Celtic Christian monks set off on the high seas in coracles, light-weight boats with wicker frames of woven saplings covered with hides, without a rudder to chart their course. Rudderless voyages were, for these adventurers, an act of faith. While they were agents of their journeys, actively responding to God's call, they trusted that God would bring their boats to their "place of resurrection," the environment best suited to deepen their faith, share the good news of God's love, and bless others—the place where they would put down roots and discover who they were really meant to be and the work they were meant to do. On high seas and lonely roadways, the Celts recognized the wildness of God's created world and the need for Divine companionship. They also trusted God's providence moving through every event and encounter. God will make a way where we see no way forward.

The Celtic spiritual adventurers delighted in the beauty of the Earth. They also knew that every day brings risk and danger as well as surprise and delight. Among the Celts, Saint Patrick is in many ways the model for an adventurous life.

Captured by pirates at age sixteen, he was impressed into slavery in Ireland. After six years, he escaped his captors and returned to his family in Britain. Safe at home, God confronted him with an unexpected adventure, the call through a dream to return to Ireland to evangelize those who had once enslaved him. Armed with God's Spirit, Patrick returned and eventually became the Bishop of Ireland.

Legend has it that, angered by Patrick's missionary zeal, a chieftain placed a price on his head. One day as Patrick was being pursued by the chieftain's minions, he prayed for deliverance and was miraculously rescued by Divine providence. His blood-thirsty pursuers heard only the cry of a deer bounding into the woods. Patrick's adventurous trust in God is reflected in the prayerful words of the Breastplate, or Deer Cry, perhaps the best-known Celtic affirmation of God's encompassing presence amid life's threats:

I arise today
With the might of heaven:
The rays of the sun,
The beams of the moon,
The glory of fire,
The speed of wind,
The depth of sea,
The stability of earth,
The hardness of rock.[6]

Patrick continues his affirmation of God's gentle yet protective and occasionally fierce providence, revealed in Christ's companionship along every step of the journey:

> *Christ behind and before me,*
> *Christ beneath and above me,*
> *Christ with me and in me,*
> *Christ around and about me,*
> *Christ on my left and on my right,*
> *Christ when I rise in the morning,*
> *Christ when I lie down at night,*
> *Christ in each heart that thinks of me,*
> *Christ in each mouth that speaks of me,*
> *Christ in each eye that sees me,*
> *Christ in each ear that hears me.*[7]

Like pilgrims and adventurers throughout the ages, Celtic Christians grounded their peregrinations in the witness of scripture: the aged Abraham and Sarah's journey to a new home, the Hebrews' sojourn to the Promised Land, Jesus' retreat in the wilderness, and Paul's missionary voyages. Today, as we go about our daily adventures, we can also remember the adventures of Mary and Joseph: the angelic visitations, the reluctant pilgrimage to Bethlehem, the quest for shelter for their child's birth, the unexpected arrival of shepherds and magi, and the flight to Egypt to ensure their child's survival.

The Celtic Christians recognized that despite the apparent stability of ordinary life, every day can be an adventure. Our best laid plans can be turned upside down by an unexpected phone call, chance encounter, or synchronous event. Daily adventures call forth a sense of the Holy not just to protect but to inspire.

I on Thy path, O God.
Thou God in my steps.
Bless me, O God,
The earth beneath my foot,
Bless me, O God,
The path whereon I go.[8]

Mother Teresa of Calcutta is said to have referred to our daily adventures as a call to do ordinary things with great love. According to her biographer Malcolm Muggeridge,

Mother Teresa asserted that our vocation is to do something beautiful for God. Every task can incarnate God's love in the world. We can choose to be God's companions in healing the Earth one act at a time.

A long-ago Celtic homemaker began the day with the following prayer:

This morning, as I kindle the fire upon my hearth,
I pray that the flame of God's love may burn in my heart,
and the hearts of all I meet today.
I pray that no envy and malice,
no hatred or fear,
may smother the flame.
I pray that indifference and apathy, contempt and pride,
may not pour like cold water on the fire.
Instead, may the spark of God's love
light the love in my heart,
that it may burn brightly through the day.
And may I warm those that are lonely,
whose hearts are cold and lifeless,
so that all may know the comfort of God's love.[9]

The Celtic practice of blessing the hands testifies to the affirmation that we are always on holy ground and that domestic tasks can be portals to Divinity. What we do really matters. In the spirit of the butterfly effect identified by meteorologists, our actions radiate across our households and the universe. An unexpected act of kindness can change the course of a human life and the history of the planet. Our lives are our gifts to God, whose own journey embraces every step we take. For those with eyes to see, God speaks through every encounter and every task. We are partners and co-creators with God in bringing beauty to the microcosm and the macrocosm.

A Celtic milkmaid found holiness in the routine and repetitive act of milking her cow, who like the milkmaid herself is an embodiment of Divine creative wisdom and wondrous love.

> *Come, Mary, and milk my cow,*
> *Come, Bride, and encompass her,*
> *Come, Columba the benign*
> *And twine thine arm around my cow.*
> *Come, Mary Virgin, to my cow,*

Come, great Bride, the beauteous,
Come, thou milk maid of Jesus Christ,
And place thine arms beneath my cow.[10]

Our daily adventures become holy adventures when we devote them to God. When we experience God in the mundane, all life becomes sacramental. Even the challenges we face awaken us to God's presence and protection.

The Celtic practice of encircling prayer, or caim, has become central to my own daily pilgrimage. As I begin the day or respond to a novel situation, I either draw a circle around myself or visualize myself encircled by God's everlasting love. I typically point my index finger to the ground or outward and then rotate three times in a clockwise direction, reciting a prayer of affirmation and protection. The encircling prayer reminds me that I am always in the circle of God's love and that nothing can separate me from the love of God. Sometimes I say a portion of Saint Patrick's prayer, invoking the reality of Christ beneath, above, and around me. Other times, I recite a prayer I have written as testimony to God's ever-present love:

Circle of love,
Open my heart.
Circle of wisdom,
Enlighten my mind.
Circle of trust,
Protect my path.
Circle of healing,
Grant me new life.

It is clear that our lives are part of a holy adventure, both joyful and perilous. We need guidance and courage to face the global and national challenges of planetary destruction, rising racism and polarization, and economic injustice, as well as the personal challenges of facing the aging process, discerning our vocations, and nurturing wholeness in our families and friendships.

Christmas is an adventurous time, and as we follow the wisdom of Celtic spiritual guides, we will experience the vocation of every moment and the beauty of each day as we embody and proclaim the Christ Child born in the world of the flesh.

Go, tell it on the mountain that Jesus Christ is born!

THE 12 DAYS OF CHRISTMAS

Days of Incarnation and Adventure

.5.
THE EVE OF ADVENTURE: CHRISTMAS EVE
DECEMBER 24

Arise, shine;
for your light
has come,
and the glory of
the LORD has
risen upon you.
For darkness
shall cover
the earth,
and thick darkness the peoples;
but the LORD will arise upon you,
and his glory will appear over you.
Nations shall come to your light,
and kings to the brightness of your dawn.

> Lift up your eyes and look around;
> they all gather together,
> they come to you;
> your sons shall come from far away,
> and your daughters shall be carried on
> their nurses' arms.
> Then you shall see and be radiant;
> your heart shall thrill and rejoice.
>
> (Isaiah 60:1–5)

> Power of the storm be thine,
> Power of moon be thine,
> Power of sun.
> Power of sea be thine,
> Power of land be thine,
> Power of heaven.
>
> (*Carmina Gadelica*)

Virtually every morning, I drive down to Craigville Beach for my sunrise beach walk. As I take my first steps, I exclaim, "This is the day that God has made, and I will rejoice and be glad in it." Despite threats to the environment and the social order, I rejoice, trusting the moral arc of history and God's gentle providence to have the final word for me and the good Earth.

This morning, I encountered a fox in the course of my peregrinations. He looked at me, I saluted him, and we both went about our business. I recalled that centuries ago, the Celtic saint Brigid also had a friendly interaction with a fox.[11] My canine friend continued feasting on some detritus left by careless beachcombers, and I continued my morning prayers.

Gazing out at sea, I pondered the similarity of our time to that of the prophet Isaiah and the Holy Family. Despite differences in the political, economic, and technological landscape, life for all of us is out of joint. Political leaders have lost their reason. Oppression and misuse of power is the norm. We feel powerless before their might.

No doubt, centuries ago, Celtic adventurers experienced the fragility of their lives when confronted by political and natural powers greater than themselves. As they set sail on the high seas, uncertain of where the waves would propel their coracles, they may have exclaimed, "God, the sea is so large and my boat is so small." Yet, they sailed, trusting the God of the Elements, the God of wind and wave, to lead them to their place of resurrection.

"Arise, shine for your light has come," urges the prophet Isaiah. "God's glory is all around you," and God will give you the insight and power to forge a new world. In the words of poet Maya Angelou, "Still I rise." We must rise, companions of foxes and the non-human world, to experience light within darkness and discover that the dark we fear also holds the womb of possibility, alternative visions to the injustice, greed, and polarization of our time. The Celts remind us that we are neither isolated nor powerless. The power of sea and storm is God's, and God gives us the power to become companions in healing the world.

On this Christmas Eve, let us remember the powers of truth, beauty, and goodness set free in our world. Let us embrace the wisdom of the much maligned Pelagius, who reminds us that heresy is often more truthful than orthodoxy in expressing God's relationship to the world. Pelagius believed in the inherent goodness of the universe and humankind, and in our ability to be God's companions in shaping history.

We are not alone and powerless. The power of wave, sunshine, earth, wind, and the energy of the Big Bang flow through us, inspiring us to become the change, as Gandhi asserts, we want to see in the world.

A CHRISTMAS PRACTICE

Psalm 36:9 proclaims, "In you [O God] is the fountain of life; in your light we see light." Today, let us experience God's light within ourselves and the world. Let it inspire us to rise up and claim our vocation as agents of Divine glory.

Take a few moments amid the busyness of Christmas preparation to pause, close your eyes, and after a taking a few deep breaths, experience God's light entering your whole being with each new breath. Let Divine light inspire, energize, and heal you. Then, as you exhale, send that healing light into the universe. While darkness is beautiful, too (and should not ever be used to denigrate persons of color), we can also celebrate light. Pause throughout the day to experience the light of God in those whom you meet, joining your light with theirs in silent blessing.

A CHRISTMAS EVE PRAYER

Light of the world, dawn in me, on me, and around me. Let me be encircled by Divine light and let that light spiral forth to give light to the world. Let your light shine through me, and enlighten and bring forth birth in the fecund womb of darkness. In Christ's Name. Amen.

.6.
THE FIRST DAY OF CHRISTMAS: CHRISTMAS DAY
DECEMBER 25

In the beginning
was the Word,
and the Word was
with God,
and the Word
was God.
He was in
the beginning
with God.
All things came into being through him,
and without him
not one thing came into being.

What has come into being
in him was life,
and the life was the light of all people.
The light shines in the darkness,
and the darkness did not overcome it. . . .
And the Word became flesh
and lived among us,
and we have seen his glory,
the glory as of a father's only son, full of
grace and truth.

(John 1:1–5, 14)

Our God, God of all persons,
God of heaven and earth,
seas and rivers,
God of sun and moon,
and of all the stars,
God of high mountains
and lowly valleys. . . .
God inspires all things,
God quickens all things.

(attributed to Saint Patrick)

The word became flesh!

Cleave the wood and I am there!

The true light enlightens everyone!

In every newborn, you can see the face of God!

We live in a God-filled universe in which God is addressing you in every face and each encounter. God is present everywhere—and in its varied manifestations, life is one, interdependent, and joined. All dualism is overcome in the Love that birthed the universe 13.7 billion years ago and births each moment of our lives.

This Christmas morning, the sounds of a souped-up engine shattered the stillness of my prayer walk. I was annoyed, hoping the driver would stay away from the beach path I was walking—but he zoomed into the beach parking lot and did a couple figure eights, engine roaring. Then he stopped, turned off his engine and looked at the Nantucket Sound. A moment later he revved his engine, and sped off in his Christmas morning toy. Could he have been lured by beauty for a brief moment? Could his quest for speed, his roar on a quiet Christmas morning have been an attempt to say, "I'm here, I matter, look at me!"

Cleave the wood and I am here. Floor your accelerator and God is present.

God comes to us in distressing disguises, Mother Teresa said. God speaks to us in voices we want to block out, inviting us to look deeper into the spirits of those around us. Like Luke Skywalker, we can find kinship and something good even in the apparently diabolical Darth Vader.

Is God present in the angry Christmas Eve tweets of the lonely occupant of the White House? Is God speaking to me through the homeless couple seeking housing on Christmas Eve? Was God asking to be noticed in the revving engine on Christmas morning?

The Incarnation is God's invitation to experience God in all things and all things in God. The Incarnation opens the doors of perception so that we experience Infinity in chance encounters and unexpected places. To the passersby, I suspect, the birth of a child in a stable meant nothing. Just another baby crying, another mouth to feed, and nothing special here.

Yet in thy dark streets shineth, the everlasting light
The hopes and fears of all the years are met in thee tonight.[12]

John Scotus Eriugena (815–877), "the Irish born Gael," saw the light of God as our ultimate and deepest reality. "Its very effusion or extension or running precedes all things and is the cause of the existence of all things and is all things."[13] The world is a theophany of Divinity. In every encounter, you are standing on Holy Ground with the option to welcome the Holy Spirit. Look deeply; see the angel in the boulder and the beauty in the geode. Look behind the bloviating politician to see a lonely quest for Christ. Seek justice, and welcome the unjust as God's beloved, too. Let Christ be all in all!

A CHRISTMAS PRACTICE

Today, look for the light of God piercing all Creation. Pray with your eyes open, noting the inner light as well as the outer disguise. Look for the Infinity of all things as you open quietly the doors of perception. Let your gaze rest on everyone you meet, if only for a moment, to see the inner beauty of all Creation, even in those who initially repel or annoy you. Throughout the day, say the affirmation, "I see God's light in everyone and everything" as a reminder to look more deeply. Vow to be a light-bearer and light-giver in every situation.

A CHRISTMAS DAY PRAYER

Light of All Lights, shine through me with healing love. Let me see light hiding in the chaos of the world and let me be a midwife of moments of light and love within all whom I encounter. In Christ's Name. Amen.

.7.
THE SECOND DAY OF CHRISTMAS
DECEMBER 26

The true light, which enlightens everyone, was coming into the world.
(John 1:9)

Yet of God's being who shall be able to speak?
Of how God is everywhere
present and invisible,
of how God fills heaven and earth
and every creature?

> ... God is everywhere, utterly vast
> and everywhere nigh at hand,
> according to God's witness;
> I am, God says,
> a God at hand and not afar off.
>
> (Columbanus[14])

God's light shines in our bodies' cells as well as our souls. The energy of love gives life and light to all. Enlightenment is the destiny of all Creation. God's saving wisdom and healing power is present in the Bethlehem stable, the Palestinian village, the pilgrim caravans coming from Central America to the United States, and the chaotic verbosity of governmental leaders.

The Celts saw Divine revelation as global. Grace and Nature manifest Divine wisdom. God speaks in the carols and lessons on Christmas Eve. God's voice is heard in Muslim calls to prayer, Hindu chants, and Buddhist scriptures. Agnostics and atheists may also voice Divine inspiration. We may turn away from Divine wisdom, but no one is left out of God's enlightening love. Our prayer is that all Creation will experience God's healing love.

Today, we remember Columbanus (543–615), Irish monk and missionary, who affirmed that "life is not a resting place, it is a road."[15] Not to be confused with Columba (Columcille), who founded the monastery at Iona, Columbanus was an adventurer who gathered twelve monks to sail across the channel from Britain to Gaul, today's France, where he founded several monasteries. Columbanus reflects the pilgrim spirit of Celtic Christianity. Trusting Christ's presence everywhere, he traveled across the sea, over hill and dale, and through the Alps to share the good news of Christ's salvation. Columbanus reminds us to be bold in our adventures, even if our journeys take us no further than our neighborhood. With Christ as our inspiration, there is always enough light for the next step of our spiritual and ethical pilgrimages.

A CHRISTMAS PRACTICE

John's Gospel proclaims that the true light enlightens everyone. We are all "saints," little Christs and large-hearted Bodhisattvas (Buddhist models of compassion) in the making. Look for God's light in yourself today. Pray for spiritual enlightenment and look for the light in others, most especially those whom you judge as alien and benighted. Let your light shine in troubled places and be a light-bearer wherever you are today. Bless everyone you meet, even if you must challenge their attitudes and behaviors. Christ was born for them, too!

A CHRISTMAS PRAYER

Lead, kindly Light, across the galaxies and in my neighborhood. Let the Christ Child enlighten my soul and help me see light hidden where others see darkness. Let me trust the long arc of your providence as I travel one step at a time in the embodiment of your Realm on earth as it is in heaven. Amen.

.8.
THE THIRD DAY OF CHRISTMAS
DECEMBER 27

In the beginning when God created the heavens and the earth, the earth was a formless void and darkness covered the face of the deep, while a wind from God swept over the face of the waters. Then God said, "Let there be light";

and there was light.
And God saw that the light was good;
and God separated the light
from the darkness.
God called the light Day,
and the darkness he called Night.
And there was evening
and there was morning,
the first day.... Then God said,
"Let us make humankind in our image,
according to our likeness;
and let them have dominion over the
fish of the sea,
and over the birds of the air,
and over the cattle,
and over all the
wild animals of the earth,
and over every creeping thing that
creeps upon the earth."
So God created humankind
in his image,
in the image of God he created them;

male and female he created them.
God saw everything that he had made,
and indeed, it was very good.
And there was evening
and there was morning,
the sixth day.
(Genesis 1:1–5, 26–27, 31)

I am the flame of fire,
blazing with passionate love;
I am the spark of light,
illuminating the deepest truth;
I am the rough ocean,
heaving with righteous anger;
I am the calm lake,
comforting the troubled breast;
I am the wild storm,
raging at human sins;
I am the gentle breeze,
blowing hope in the saddened heart;
I am the dry dust,
choking worldly ambition;

> I am the wet earth,
> bearing fruits of grace.
>
> (Robert Van de Weyer[16])

Many people see the Genesis story in dualistic terms, believing that the Creation narrative is about human uniqueness and separation from the non-human world. They believe our role is to dominate the soulless world around us. Beliefs have consequences—and dualism and domination have led to destroying the foundations of life on our planet and the extinction of unique and beautiful reflections of Divine creativity.

Genesis is really about Incarnation, the ongoing creativity of God in the universe and our planet. The universe is the "maternity ward" of Divine beauty. As the philosopher Alfred North Whitehead avers, the aim of the universe is at the production of beauty. Humans are unique in giftedness but not set apart. We are part of the evolving universe and the adventurous Earth. We stand on the shoulders of Divine creativity, expressed in the interplay of wisdom, freedom, and chance embodied in dinosaurs, apes, and our primitive ancestors, supported by the flora and fauna of this good Earth. Yes, God loves the fetus; but just as important to God is the Right whale swimming off Cape Cod, with fewer than five hundred left on the planet, the victims of whaling and sea debris.

Creation leads to ethics. Love God in "the world of the flesh," T.S. Eliot counsels. Claim your role as God's companion in bringing healing and beauty to the wondrous, wild, and beautiful world of which you are a part.

Saint Kevin (498?–618), founder of the monastery at Glendalough, Ireland, has been described as the Saint Francis of the Celts. He experienced Divine artistry in a human face and a flying bird. Stories of his intimacy with the non-human world abound. According to one story, he dropped his prayer book in a pond, but before he could jump into retrieve it, an otter grasped it and placed it in his hands. Birds often perched on his shoulders when he was at prayer. Once while praying, Kevin discovered a bird had built a nest on his outstretched hand. Filled with compassion, he remained completely still, enraptured in God, until the chicks hatched.

Kevin awakens us to a world of praise, reflective of the wonder and wildness of Creation. The stories of his life invite us to see the non-human world as beloved companions, worthy of respect and ethical consideration.

A CHRISTMAS PRACTICE

Today, I invite you to walk like a Celt! Bathe your senses in the beauty of earth, water, and sky. Let the wind in the trees, the sough of waves, or the ripple of river water be your mantra; let the scent of leaf and soil be your incense; let the Earth be your support and the sun your warmth. Wherever you are, beauty surrounds you, even in urban areas. If you're able, walk with an openness to whatever you experience. City sounds can be a symphony, urban graffiti can be a tapestry, subway walls can communicate prophetic messages, and a garden patch may reveal itself at the edge of the sidewalk. Open to life in its variety, revealing the handiwork of the God of the Elements.

A CHRISTMAS PRAYER

Open my senses to experience your presence in every encounter. Let the world be a theophany, inspiring amazement, and let me treasure and nurture this good Earth. In the name of the Earth Maker. Amen.

.9.
THE FOURTH DAY OF CHRISTMAS
DECEMBER 28

In the sixth month the angel Gabriel was sent by God to a town in Galilee called Nazareth, to a virgin engaged to a man whose name was Joseph, of the house of David. The virgin's name was Mary.

And he came to her and said, "Greetings, favored one! The Lord is with you."

But she was much perplexed by his words and pondered what sort of greeting this might be. The angel said to her, "Do not be afraid, Mary, for you have found favor with God. And now, you will conceive in your womb and bear a son, and you will name him Jesus. He will be great, and will be called the Son of the Most High, and the Lord God will give to him the throne of his ancestor David. He will reign over the house of Jacob forever, and of his kingdom there will be no end."

Mary said to the angel, "How can this be, since I am a virgin?"

The angel said to her, "The Holy Spirit will come upon you, and the power of the Most High will overshadow you; therefore the child to be born will be holy; he will be called Son of God. And now, your relative Elizabeth in her old age has also conceived a son; and this is the sixth month for her who was said to be barren. For nothing will be impossible with God."

Then Mary said, "Here am I, the servant of the Lord; let it be with me according to your word." Then the angel departed from her.

(Matthew 1:26–37)

> What is the fruit of study?
> To perceive the eternal Word of God
> reflected in every plant and insect,
> every bird and animal,
> and every man and woman.
>
> (St. Ninian's Catechism, 5th-century[17])

Today, we affirm the interplay of Divine call and human response. The angel Gabriel presents young Mary with an impossible possibility, to be the unwed mother of God's Chosen Child. In the midst of ordinary life, the veil between heaven and earth is pierced and shafts of Divine light, as

Pelagius asserted, envelope Mary, mystically calling her to an adventure uncharted by any woman or man in history, embodying Divinity in human flesh.

What if Mary had said "no" to the angelic invitation? Was Mary the first young woman addressed by Gabriel? Did another woman say "no"?

In her exchange with Gabriel, despite being overwhelmed by her angelic visitor, Mary maintains her agency and ability to shape Divine revelation in her uniquely human way. Jesus was God embodied, and at the same time, he was influenced by his mother, genetically, emotionally, and spiritually in utero and throughout his life.

God calls us to be creative too. God invites our uniquely personal response to give birth to holiness and beauty in our world. The Divine encourages our freedom and creativity, and calls us to the high adventure of companionship in healing the world.

Today, we are grateful for the spiritual leadership of Hilda (614–668), founding abbess of the monastery at Whitby, a "double monastery" composed of women and men under her spiritual direction. Born into royalty, Hilda felt the call to discipleship and simplicity of life. She is best known as a patron of the arts, encouraging poets and bards, most notably Caedmon. Her support of Celtic poetry, especially following the hostile Roman takeover of the Celtic church, enabled Celtic literature to survive and flourish despite Roman Catholic strictures.

God is experienced as fully in music, poetry, literature, and the visual arts as in religious ritual, scripture, and theological reflection.

A CHRISTMAS PRACTICE

African American mystic and theologian Howard Thurman asserted that the world is saved by the singing of the angels. Divine messengers encounter us in many shapes, shifting to meet our needs and experiences. Today, open your senses to Divine visitations and their call to you. Pray that the doors of perception be cleansed, so that you experience the Infinity of all things and follow God's wisdom in exploring your own gifts and possibilities.

A CHRISTMAS PRAYER

Holy One, whose angels guide my steps, unbeknownst to me, let me say "yes" to today's invitation to birthing and creativity. Let me respond to your call to be your companion in birthing love and beauty in the world. In the Name of Mary's Baby. Amen.

.10.
THE FIFTH DAY OF CHRISTMAS
DECEMBER 29

In those days Mary set out and went with haste to a Judean town in the hill country, where she entered the house of Zechariah and greeted Elizabeth.

When Elizabeth heard Mary's greeting, the child leaped in her womb. And Elizabeth was filled with the Holy Spirit and exclaimed with a loud cry, "Blessed are you among women, and blessed is the fruit of your womb. And why has this happened to me, that the mother of my Lord comes to me? For as soon as I heard the sound of your greeting, the child in my womb leaped for joy."

(Matthew 1:39–45)

> Your Creation is a million wondrous miracles, beautiful to behold.
> I ask of you just one more miracle,
> beautify my soul.
>
> (Robert Van de Weyer[18])

Poet Walt Whitman wrote, "All is miracle"—and that affirmation is at the heart of today's readings. John leaps for joy in utero. Divine revelation shines in the womb and in all Creation.

The conception of the sixth-century Celtic saint known as both Mungo and Kentigern was the result of his mother's rape—and yet, according to tradition, he was blessed and called by God while still in his mother's womb. Fetal revelation is not exceptional to the Celts and to mystics throughout history. The psalmist writes, "it was you who formed my inward parts; you knit me together in my mother's womb" (139:13).

Psalm 148 describes a world of praise in which all Creation glorifies its Creator—sun, moon, and stars; snow and hail; plants and people; companion animals and sea monsters. The Psalms end with the command, "Let everything that breathes praise God!" (Psalm 150:6).

What would it be like to live in a world of praise? What wisdom would we gain from the insight that everything from fetuses to Right whales and hammerhead sharks touches and is touched by God? How would this change our attitudes toward the non-human world, the care of refugee children, and the challenging interplay of fetal and women's rights? Reverence for life, as Albert Schweitzer asserted, is the primary response to the wonder of Creation, even when we need to make difficult decisions of national security, personal ethics, and economic justice.

All Creation, fetuses and mothers, friends and enemies, pangolins and presidents, experiences God at its depths and deserves our care. In the complexities of life, let us delight in Creation and honor the experience of all God's human and non-human children.

Ita of Killeedy (died 570) founded a small community of nuns in County Limerick. She was the spiritual mentor of both the adventurous Brendan, who sought her spiritual guidance between voyages, and Saint Mungo's foster father, a wonder-working abbot named Serf. Ita reminds us of the importance of spiritual guidance and mentoring, selflessly encouraging the next generation to explore its gifts and talents, and chart its own adventures to places beyond the mentor's own experience.

Mentoring and spiritual guidance is grounded in reverence for those whose lives are placed in our care. Like the gift of Anam Cara friendship, mentoring enables those with whom we interact to experience the holiness, wonder, and giftedness of their own lives as blessings to the world. Joyful companionship leads to seeing traces of Divinity in everyone we meet.

A CHRISTMAS PRACTICE

John's fetal response invites us to care for pregnant women and young children, near and far. Bless every

parent and child you encounter, whether in person or on the news. Look beyond borders to care for children in distant lands and pilgrim caravans. Discover Jesus and John in the face of every child. Let this discovery awaken you to prayerful and supportive relationships and political responses that honor the lives of children and mothers everywhere.

A CHRISTMAS PRAYER

"Bless all the dear children in your tender care." O Loving Mother of Creation, let us be midwives of holiness and health in our teaching, mentoring, parenting and grandparenting, caring, and political involvement. Help us to glorify you as we honor each child and parent, as well as the child in ourselves. Let us leap for joy at your Incarnation in this good Earth. In the Name of the Mother of us all. Amen.

.11.

THE SIXTH DAY OF CHRISTMAS

DECEMBER 30

And Mary said,
"My soul magnifies the Lord,
and my spirit rejoices in God my Savior,
for he has looked with favor
on the lowliness of his servant.
Surely, from now on all generations
will call me blessed;

for the Mighty One has done
great things for me,
and holy is his name.
His mercy is for those who fear him
from generation to generation.
He has shown strength with his arm;
he has scattered the proud in the
thoughts of their hearts.
He has brought down the powerful
from their thrones,
and lifted up the lowly;
he has filled the hungry
with good things,
and sent the rich away empty."

(Luke 1:46–53)

I should like a lake of finest ale
for the king of kings.
I should like a table of the choicest food
for the family of heaven.
Let the ale be made
from the fruits of the earth

and the food be forgiving love.
I should welcome the poor to my feast,
for they are God's children.
I should welcome the sick to my feast,
for they are God's joy.
Let the poor sit with Jesus
at the highest place,
and the sick dance with the angels.
God bless the poor, God bless the sick,
and bless our human race.
God bless our food, God bless our drink.
All homes, O God, embrace.

(adapted from a prayer attributed to Saint Brigid[19])

What we need today is prophetic healing. We need lifestyles and governmental policies that ensure the well-being of every child and the dignity of every stranger. Mary's Magnificat (Luke 1:46–53), which is anything but meek and mild, invites this radical change into our world. She calls for turning the world upside down so that it can be right side up in God's eyes.

Christmas is profoundly political. Jesus is born in Bethlehem as the result of Roman oppression, including the need for revenue to support Roman building projects and the Roman occupying force. This means that Jesus never spent one day as a free person. He could have been impressed into duty by a Roman soldier merely by the military's whim. As spiritual teacher Howard Thurman said, Jesus' people lived with their back against the wall—not unlike today's political refugees, the homeless of our cities, the hopeless of Appalachia, or the parents and children separated from each other by political decision makers.

In the context of political disenfranchisement, income inequality, and governmental violence, Mary channels God's vision for humanity. She challenges us to incarnate Jesus' vision as our gift to God this Christmas season. Planetary and personal survival demand a change of heart and changes in our political and economic priorities. We can't wait, Mary counsels, for other nations or our neighbors to turn from the ways of death to the path of life. We need to be pioneers of God's Shalom in our time. While politicians crow about saying "Merry Christmas," we need to remember that Christmas is more than words; it is the embodiment of God's love to heal the world.

With great joy, we remember today Brigid of Kildare, "the cell of the oaks," whose life spanned the fifth and sixth centuries. She was someone who was not only a bridge between centuries but also between cultures and spiritual traditions, a pioneer in what today we call interspirituality or spiritual fluidity.

Brigid, whose feast day is February 1, the Druidic holy day of Imbolc, was the daughter of a Druid chieftain and a Christian servant, who worked in her father's dairy. She was known for her generosity and concern for the poor, inspired by her affirmation, "I feed the poor in the name of Christ, for Christ is in the body of every poor person."[20] Brigid, known as "Mary of the Gaels," scandalized her father and turned her world upside down by placing the needs of others ahead of her own comfort. Her wealth was a conduit of blessing to persons experiencing poverty, and according to generations of oral tradition, God always multiplied her gifts so that her generosity was amplified to bless others.

According to legend, Brigid was a joyful soul who was able to turn water into beer, reserving the miracle of water into wine for the Savior. As abbess of a "double monastery," she guided the spiritual journeys of both men and women. Like

Hilda and Ita, she reminds us of the importance of women in shaping the Christian faith, yesterday, today, and tomorrow

A CHRISTMAS PRACTICE

How and where can you give the "finest ale" to God's needy people? Perhaps pray with your hands and wallet as you buy groceries to donate to the food pantry or local soup kitchen. Consider volunteering to enable the vulnerable to experience more abundant life.

A CHRISTMAS PRAYER

Let me share my life and love with all Creation, see you in the neglected and vulnerable, and share my gifts with a wise and generous heart. In Jesus' Name. Amen.

.12.
THE SEVENTH DAY OF CHRISTMAS
DECEMBER 31

Now the birth of Jesus the Messiah took place in this way. When his mother Mary had been engaged to Joseph, but before they lived together, she was found to be with child from the Holy Spirit. Her husband Joseph, being a righteous man and unwilling to expose her to public disgrace, planned to dismiss her quietly. But just when he had resolved to do this, an angel of the Lord appeared to him in a dream and said, "Joseph, son of David, do not be afraid to take Mary as your wife, for the child conceived in her is from the Holy Spirit. She will bear a son, and you are to name him Jesus, for he will save his people from their sins.". . . When Joseph awoke from sleep, he did as the angel of the Lord commanded him; he took her as his wife, but had no marital relations with her until she had borne a son; and he named him Jesus.

(Matthew 1:18–21, 24–25)

> Christ behind and before me,
> Christ beneath and above me,
> Christ with me and in me,
> Christ around and about me,
> Christ on my left and on my right,
> Christ when I rise in the morning,

> Christ when I lie down at night,
> Christ in each heart that thinks of me,
> Christ in each mouth that speaks of me,
> Christ in each eye that sees me,
> Christ in each ear that hears me.
>
> (attributed to Saint Patrick[21])

A dream can change everything! God gave Joseph a large and impossible dream that opened up the horizons of Incarnation on our planet. Mary said "yes" to an angel, and Joseph said "yes" to a dream. The future depends on big dreams that we can embody in our daily lives, as well as in community and political involvement.

Carl Jung reminded us that dreams can reveal God working through the unconscious to challenge our current lifestyles, reorient our spiritual GPS, and alert us to our authentic vocations. God gives us gentle visions and dreams, quiet invitations, moment by moment and over the long vistas of our lives. Awakening to and discerning our dreams opens the door to a lifelong holy adventure.

What dream is God giving you today? What dream is God presenting to your congregation or community group?

What is the real dream beneath the American dream that God is giving our nation today?

Patrick, who lived during the fifth century, is synonymous with Celtic Christianity in the eyes of many persons. Living in what is now Britain, at sixteen years of age Patrick was captured by Irish pirates and sold into slavery, where he worked as a shepherd. After six years in servitude, a Divine voice announced that his ship was waiting and that now was the time to flee Ireland.

Safe at home again, Patrick's plans were changed once more by a vision—a God-given dream—of an Irish man begging him to return to the land of his servitude. Following God's voice, Patrick returned to Ireland, where he spent the remaining years of his life preaching the gospel.[22]

Patrick's best-known prayer is the Lorica, or Breastplate, which invokes God's protection. It reminds us that Christ encircles us wherever we are. We are always in the care of a loving God, who guides, inspires, and protects—a God who sometimes sends dreams to wake us up!

A CHRISTMAS PRACTICE

Today, I want to share two practices. First, take time today to live with Patrick's prayer, written at the beginning of this chapter. Experience Christ surrounding, protecting, and guiding you in every moment of life. See yourself encircled by God's presence and providence. Second, ask God to enable you to experience, remember, and act on life-transforming dreams: "What is your dream for me? Where is your Spirit calling me forward to new adventures? What deep mystery can I experience that will help me receive your healing and transformation?"

A CHRISTMAS PRAYER

Give me, O God, a dream to remember, a dream that awakens me from spiritual slumber and sets my feet on your high adventure. In the Name of the Cosmic Dreamer. Amen.

.13.
THE EIGHTH DAY OF CHRISTMAS
JANUARY 1

In those days a decree went out from Emperor Augustus that all the world should be registered. This was the first registration and was taken while Quir-
inius was governor of Syria. All went to their own towns to be registered. Joseph also went from the town of Nazareth in Galilee to Judea, to the city of David called Bethlehem, because he was

descended from the house and family of David. He went to be registered with Mary, to whom he was engaged and who was expecting a child. While they were there, the time came for her to deliver her child. And she gave birth to her firstborn son and wrapped him in bands of cloth, and laid him in a manger, because there was no place for them in the inn.

(Luke 2:1–7)

> The God of the Element's guarding,
> The loving Christ's guarding,
> The Holy Spirit's guarding,
> Be cherishing me, be aiding me.
>
> (traditional Celtic prayer[23])

"Out with the old, in with the new!" So goes a popular New Year's affirmation. The birth of Jesus integrates something old and something new. It injects a new possibility, the Word and Wisdom made flesh in the messiness of our world—God embodied in history, flesh and bone revealing the heart of

God. The birth of Jesus also reflects the ancient and universal story of Divine presence. Many centuries before the birth of Jesus, God providentially guided the human story. Long before humankind even came on the scene, God moved through the energy of the Big Bang to set the stage for cosmic and planetary evolution.

The birth of Jesus unites spirituality and politics. Jesus is born in an occupied land, not unlike today's Palestine, and Jesus confronts the Herods of his time just as we must confront the Herods of our own. The Christ takes flesh in the challenges of human history, humbly in a stable, among the forgotten peoples of the world. Jesus is among the homeless and oppressed as well as the affluent and powerful. His birth challenges us to embrace God's novel possibilities in our time: the dream of Shalom, of wholeness for all people; the eclipse of nationalism by world loyalty; the transcendence of race and sexuality by the rainbow community of God's love.

Today, we honor Darlughdach, the sixth-century nun who served as Brigid's ambassador and as her Anam Cara. According to legend, the two women were so spiritually intimate that they shared a bed, leading some contemporary scholars to suggest that their love sprung from the whole person, body, mind, and spirit. These two Anam Caras remind us that spiritual friendship is a great gift. The mirroring of spirits enables us to experience the face of God in ourselves and others.

According to tradition, when Brigid told her dear companion of her impending death, Darlughdach asked to die with her. Brigid refused to grant her wish, asking her to lead the abbey for one year. Brigid died on February 1, 525, the feast of Imbolc, the festival of the Druidic goddess Brigid. On February 1, 526, exactly one year later, Darlughdach died, fulfilling her promise to Brigid.

In recent years, Brigid and Darlughdach have been claimed as patron saints of the LGBTQ+ community, in recognition of their unique friendship and the love of God that heals those who have been marginalized and traumatized by religious institutions. They are models of a new humanity, embodying a spiritual adventure in which all are pilgrims and none are strangers.

New Year's Day reminds us that we ourselves are the very ones we have been waiting for, as June Jordan asserted. This year, we are invited to become the horizon of hope of a new world, in which God's will is embodied on earth as it is in heaven.

A CHRISTMAS PRACTICE

Let New Year's Day invite you to embody God's horizon of hope in your daily life. What new practice—prayer, meditation, service—can you embody to transform your world? In what ways can you integrate God's vision for the new year into your daily life? In what ways can you embody the changes you want to see in the world?

A CHRISTMAS PRAYER

God of ages past and hopes to come, awaken me to the Holy Here-and-Now and the Lively Future you envision for me. Help me join my care for myself, family, friends, and nation with a deeper world loyalty, embracing your entire beloved Creation. In the name of the Ever-New God. Amen.

.14.
THE NINTH DAY OF CHRISTMAS
JANUARY 2

In that region there were shepherds living in the fields, keeping watch over their flock by night. Then an angel of the Lord stood before them, and the glory of the Lord shone around them, and they were terrified. But the angel said to them, "Do not be afraid; for see—I am bringing you good news of great joy for all the people: to you is born this day in the city of David a Savior, who is the Messiah, the Lord. This will be a sign for you: you will find a child wrapped in bands of cloth and lying in a manger." And suddenly there was with the angel a multitude of the heavenly host, praising God and saying,

> "Glory to God in the highest heaven,
> and on earth peace
> among those whom he favors!"

When the angels had left them and gone into heaven, the shepherds said to one another, "Let us go now to Bethlehem and see this thing that has taken place, which the Lord has made known to us." So they went with haste and found Mary and Joseph, and the child lying in the manger. When they saw this, they made known what had been told them about this child; and all who heard it were amazed at what the shepherds told them. But Mary treasured all these words and pondered them in her heart. The shepherds returned, glorifying and praising God for all they had heard and seen, as it had been told them.

(Luke 2:8–20)

Let us go forth,
In the goodness of our Merciful Father,
In the gentleness of our Brother Jesus,
In the radiance of his Holy Spirit....
Let us go forth in
The wisdom of the all-seeing Father,
In the patience of our all-loving Brother,
In the truth of our all-knowing Spirit....
Such is the path
for all servants of Christ,
The path from death to eternal life.

(Celtic prayer[24])

Howard Thurman asserts that "there must be always remaining in every [person's] life some place for the singing of the angels." Amid the confusion, crassness, and complexity of life, "life is saved by the singing of angels."[25]

Angels, messengers of God, are at the heart of the Christmas stories, revealing God's desire to reach out to humankind in healing and life-transforming ways. In the biblical tradition and throughout history, angels come to us in forms we need, presenting us with the messages we need to hear in this moment of time. Angels remind us that we are never alone and without resource. God is with us providing us with everything we need to flourish and bless the world.

Could an angel be reaching out to you at this moment? Could an angel be providing you with guidance and insight, inviting you to realize your current calling as God's companion in blessing the world? Open your senses and you might hear the singing of angels.

Today, we give thanks for Aidan of Landisfarne (died 651), whose humble approach to evangelism restored the Christian faith to Northumbria. In counseling monks under his care, Aidan advised, "If you are to meet people, you are to have your feet on the ground" not on horseback, to meet them as equals rather than superiors.[26] Aidan saw relationship as the heart of sharing God's good news.

We all come as equals before God, standing with all people as recipients of God's love and needing God's grace. Just as angels come to us in ways that we need, our calling is to reach out to our neighbors in ways that they need and not as intellectual or spiritual superiors.

Aidan saw walking in the spirit of Jesus as the avenue to reach those beyond the faith. Every moment provided the opportunity for Aidan to praise God, including the hour of death. On his deathbed, Aiden whispered "Jesus, Jesus, Jesus." When a young monk encouraged him to rest quietly, the monk replied, "I have loudly proclaimed Christ with my whole life. If I cannot shout his name, I will whisper it."[27]

Perhaps angels sometimes whisper their messages to us—and they, like Aidan, proclaim to us the identity of the Divine.

A CHRISTMAS PRACTICE

Today, let us listen for the singing for the angels. While God comes to us intimately and directly, we can also ask for angelic visitations to show us the way and awaken us to service. Let us be open to "angels unaware" as they cross our path every day.

A CHRISTMAS PRAYER

Holy One, come to us in your many manifestations. Awaken our senses to Divine messages in every encounter and give us the insight and courage to follow God's way. In Christ's Name.

.15.
THE TENTH DAY OF CHRISTMAS
JANUARY 3

Now there was a man in Jerusalem whose name was Simeon; this man was righteous and devout, looking forward to the consolation of Israel, and the Holy Spirit rested on him. It had been revealed to him by the Holy Spirit that he would not see death before he had seen the Lord's Messiah. Guided by the

Spirit, Simeon came into the temple; and when the parents brought in the child Jesus, to do for him what was customary under the law, Simeon took him in his arms and praised God, saying, "Master, now you are dismissing your servant in peace, according to your word; for my eyes have seen your salvation, which you have prepared in the presence of all peoples, a light for revelation to the Gentiles and for glory to your people Israel.". . .

There was also a prophet, Anna the daughter of Phanuel, of the tribe of Asher. She was of a great age, having lived with her husband seven years after her marriage, then as a widow to the age of eighty-four. She never left the temple but worshiped there with fasting and prayer night and day. At that moment she came, and began to praise God and to speak about the child to all who were looking for the redemption of Jerusalem.

(Luke 2:22–32, 36–40)

I am the wave on the ocean,
I am the murmur of leaves rustling,
I am the rays of the sun,
I am the beam of moon and stars,
I am the power of trees growing.
I am the bud breaking into blossom,
I am the movement
of salmon swimming,
I am the courage
of the wild boar fighting,
I am the speed of the stag running,
I am the strength
of the ox pulling the plough,
I am the size of the mighty oak tree,
And I am the thoughts of all people
Who praise my beauty and grace.

(adapted from the "Song of Amergin"[28])

Thin places everywhere! Still, sometimes you need to travel the high seas to find your place of resurrection. Other times it's right where you are, ushering you into God's magic realm. Simeon and Anna took a journey without distance. They were waiting for God's revelation, but their waiting was active and prayerful. They trained their eyes to recognize God's presence amid the hubbub of the Temple visitors.

The realm of God is within us and among us and around us, in the stag, ox, mighty tree, and your own deepest reflections. All the wonders you seek, and the inspiration you crave, are right where you are, within your own personal experience. Thin places, holy isles, burning bushes, angelic songs, and magi bearing gifts are everywhere when we open our eyes, and experience the Infinity of Life. It's a matter of waiting, with Simeon and Anna: pausing, breathing deeply, opening your senses, and experiencing this Holy Here-and-Now. Pause awhile and know that God's thin place is right here, right now, in this holy place and time.

As we go about our daily rounds, we need to embrace the wisdom of Brendan the Navigator (484–577), who earned the title through his amazing sea voyage, stretching over seven years and thousands of miles from Ireland to (possibly)

Greenland or Newfoundland, Canada. On the way, in search of a holy island, God's place of resurrection and new life, Brendan and his crew had great adventures and met strange beasts, whales, and sea serpents.[29] C.S. Lewis said that Brendan's voyages inspired one of his own Narnia tales, *The Voyage of the Dawn Treader*, and in particular, the character Reepicheep, the gallant mouse who searches for Aslan's country.

Brendan inspires our daily pilgrimages, reminding us that God is our companion and guide in every encounter and event. Every wave, circumstance, and person bring us closer to God. Life is a holy adventure whether on the high seas, driving a child to soccer practice, or sitting in meditation.

A CHRISTMAS PRACTICE

Jesus told his followers to ask, seek, and knock. In this practice, begin by asking for your senses to be opened to holiness and remind yourself throughout the day that your calling is to seek God in all things and all things in God. Pause and breathe deeply, seeking to see more deeply the persons around you. Knock on the doors of the familiar, finding the Divine in your beloved friends, family, and neighborhood.

A CHRISTMAS PRAYER

Remind me to seek you patiently, Loving God, so that I might experience thin places everywhere and bring forth beauty and love wherever I find myself. In Christ's Name. Amen.

.16.
THE ELEVENTH DAY OF CHRISTMAS
JANUARY 4

Now after [the magi] had left, an angel of the Lord appeared to Joseph in a dream and said, "Get up, take the child and his mother, and flee to Egypt, and remain there until I tell you; for Herod is about

to search for the child, to destroy him."
Then Joseph got up, took the child and
his mother by night, and went to Egypt,
and remained there until the death
of Herod.

(Matthew 2:13–15)

> I am bathing my face
> In the mild rays of the sun
> As Mary washed Christ
> In the rich milk of Egypt.
> Sweetness be in my mouth,
> Wisdom be in my speech,
> The love the fair Mary gave her Son
> May I see at the center of all life.
>
> (*Carmina Gadelica*[30])

Jesus, Mary, and Joseph were political refugees. Behind the glorious story of God taking flesh in human life is the painful reality of political violence and asylum-seeking. Whether in Syria, the US borderlands, Yemen, or Myanmar, innocent children are still the primary victims of political power plays.

Perhaps the Holy Family joined a pilgrim caravan looking for safety in Egypt. Like the Hebrews in the age of Pharaoh, they may have been met with fear and suspicion. Like refugees throughout history, they depended on the kindness of strangers.

The flight of the Holy Family asks us to reshape our understanding of Christmas. Welcoming the Christ Child means making a place for strangers, immigrants, and asylum seekers. National security and citizenship are important values, but Jesus the refugee child invites us to open our hearts and shape our political policies to ensure that every child, regardless of national origin, is treated as a little Christ. Christmas takes us beyond tribe and nation to embrace the holiness of others, in our personal and political lives, as the earliest forms of Celtic Christianity sought to embrace the indigenous Druids.

Columba (also called Columcille; 521–597) inspires us to discover thin and sacred places everywhere. After becoming embroiled in a political conflict, Columba was exiled to Scotland, where he established a monastery on the isle of Iona. He knew firsthand the pain the Holy Family felt as they fled their homeland. He also knew that God could be found in a foreign land. Like Francis and Kevin, Columba had a particular affinity with the non-human world, forging intimate relations with birds and livestock. While on a visit to Scottish mainland, Columba encountered some residents there who were burying a man attacked and drowned by a ferocious "water beast." Columba made the sign of the cross, bid the water beast leave the shoreland, and the beast was never seen again. Some commentators suggest that Columba's prayer may have banished the legendary Loch Ness Monster.

Columba referred to Christ as his arch-Druid. By using the language and insights of another faith tradition, Columba serves as a guide for our responses to the spiritual and ethnic pluralism of our time, in which many people are spiritually fluid or interspiritual, integrating multiple spiritual practices in their daily lives. Christ is the way that excludes no ways (as theologian John Cobb asserts). Christ does not negate other spiritual paths but instead enlivens and enlightens them.

Columba was a mystic-scholar. It is said that he never went more than an hour without prayer and study, alerting us to the importance of study as a form of prayer. He challenges us to not only love God with our hearts but also with our minds.

A CHRISTMAS PRACTICE

Prayerfully explore how you can provide spiritual sanctuary to strangers and immigrants in our midst. While there are many welcoming responses, at the very least we must challenge the demonization of refugees as well as publicly promoted fallacies about their origins or motivations. Explore what you might do to provide hospitality to immigrants. Make a commitment to see Christ in immigrants—as well as in those who demonize and misrepresent them.

A CHRISTMAS PRAYER

Let me make a home for you, Jesus. Show me ways to open my heart, arms, and resources to provide well-being for the marginalized and those who dwell in the shadows for fear of being deported. Let

me, regardless of my political position, be guided by compassion and truth, not fear and falsehood. In the name of the Refugee Christ. Amen.

.17.
THE TWELFTH DAY OF CHRISTMAS
JANUARY 5

When Herod saw that he had been tricked by the wise men, he was infuriated, and he sent and killed all the children in and around Bethlehem who were two years old or under, according to the time that he had learned from the wise men. Then was fulfilled what had been spoken through the prophet Jeremiah:

> "A voice was heard in Ramah,
> wailing and loud lamentation,
> Rachel weeping for her children;
> she refused to be consoled, because
> they are no more."

When Herod died, an angel of the Lord suddenly appeared in a dream to Joseph in Egypt and said, "Get up, take the child and his mother, and go to the land of Israel, for those who were seeking the child's life are dead." Then Joseph got up, took the child and his mother, and went to the land of Israel. But when he heard that Archelaus was ruling over Judea in place of his father Herod, he was afraid to go there. And after being warned in a dream, he went away to the district of Galilee. There he made his home in a town called Nazareth, so that what had been spoken through the prophets might be fulfilled, "He will be called a Nazarene."

(Matthew 2:16–23)

> I arise today
> through a mighty strength,
> the invocation of the Trinity,
> through belief in the threeness,
> through confession of the oneness
> of the Creator of Creation.
> I arise today
> through the strength of Christ's birth
> with his baptism,
> through the strength of his crucifixion
> with his burial,
> through the strength
> of his resurrection with his ascension.
> I arise today
> through God's strength to pilot me:
> God's might to uphold me,
> God's hand to guard me,

> God's shield to protect me,
> God's ear to hear me,
> God's host to save me ...
> from all who shall wish me ill,
> afar and anear,
> alone and in a multitude.
>
> (attributed to Saint Patrick[31])

Jesus' safety is bought with a price—the death of infants and toddlers in Bethlehem. Did Mary feel guilty, do you think? Was she burdened by grief at the death of children, many of whose parents were her friends?

The Christmas story is profoundly realistic. Kings and national leaders will condone or even authorize the deaths of children to pursue their own political objectives. Fear-based ideologies trump flesh-and-blood humans. Little children are pawns in a game of thrones in which victory often goes to the most ruthless and heartless combatants.

But there is another way, the Christmas message affirms. This is the way of the Prince of Peace, whose power is guided by justice and love. Spiritual power is relational not unilateral. It listens before it acts, and in its quest of Shalom it takes into consideration the well-being of strangers and opponents.

Power can be creative and life-supportive. It need not be domineering or destructive. The Incarnation models healing power and loving power, God with us feeling our pain and responding with love. Following the Christ Child inspires us to empower relationships that promote well-being for the greatest number of people and for the planet, given the concrete realities we must face. Power can heal, protect, nurture, and balance community and personal survival with world loyalty.

On the eve of Epiphany, we remember a more recent Celtic mystic, Alexander John Scott (1805–1866) who counseled people to listen for God in all things, "in the growth of the tree, in the rising of the morning sun, in the stars at night, and in the moon."[32] Scott was accused of heresy due to his belief that God loves all Creation, with no one and no thing excluded. God's love, Scott insisted, embraces all humankind, and God's spirit is "impregnated throughout all Creation."[33] God is not just beside us or above us, but within us. The reality of God's ubiquitous presence inspired Scott to be a leader in the Christian Socialist movement, working to ensure the use of power to promote the well-being of all God's beloved children.

Today, Scott reminds us that incarnational theology leads to compassionate ethics, embracing both all humankind and the non-human world.

A CHRISTMAS PRACTICE

Many people are familiar with Tibetan prayer flags as a way of interceding for the world. The Celts had a similar practice of creating "clooties" (rags or cloths) as a means of multiplying our prayers. Often placed on trees near wells, these prayer cloths or flags were part of a healing ritual, involving shedding the ills of the past. As they disintegrated, so did one's suffering. Today, at the eve of Epiphany, we remember the massacre of the infants or innocents, often celebrated on December 28, and pray for the children who are "massacred" every

day by the powers and principalities of the world—in Yemen, Syria, Sudan, on the borderlands, and in urban and rural neighborhoods of the United States. Create a simple "clootie" and hang it on a tree or home fixture, drawing or attaching a picture of a child or other prayer concern. Let your prayers flow into the universe, companioning with God's quest for a world in which laughter and play characterize the life of all God's children.

A CHRISTMAS PRAYER

Holy One, bless the children and the child in me. Let the Christ Child in Bethlehem inspire me to welcome the child in my heart, to speak for the refugee, to reach out to the forgotten, and work for the coming of Shalom for every child. In the name of the Refugee Jesus. Amen.

.18.
THE FEAST OF EPIPHANY
JANUARY 6

In the time of King Herod, after Jesus was born in Bethlehem of Judea, wise men from the East came to Jerusalem, asking, "Where is the child who has been born king of the Jews? For we observed his star at its rising, and have come to pay him homage." When King Herod heard this, he was frightened, and all Jerusalem with him; and calling together all the chief priests and scribes of the people, he inquired of them where the Messiah was to be born. They told him, "In Bethlehem of Judea; for so it has been written by the prophet:

> 'And you, Bethlehem,
> in the land of Judah,
> are by no means
> least among the rulers of Judah;
> for from you shall come a ruler
> who is to shepherd my people Israel.'"

Then Herod secretly called for the wise men and learned from them the exact time when the star had appeared. Then he sent them to Bethlehem, saying, "Go and search diligently for the child; and when you have found him, bring me word so that I may also go and pay him homage." When they had heard the king, they set out; and there, ahead of them, went the star that they had seen at its rising, until it stopped over the place where the child was. When they saw that the star had stopped, they were overwhelmed with joy. On entering the house, they saw the child with Mary his mother; and they knelt down and paid him homage. Then, opening their treasure chests, they offered him gifts of gold, frankincense, and myrrh. And having been warned in a dream not to return to Herod, they left for their own country by another road.

(Matthew 2:7–12)

> I on thy path, O God.
> Thou God in my steps.
> Bless me, O God,
> The earth beneath my foot,
> Bless me, O God,
> The path whereon I go.
> (*Carmina Gadelica*[34])

Christmas is a never-ending story. What we may think of as the "end" of Christmas marks the beginning of Epiphany, the celebration of God's revelation in the holy otherness of ethnic, cultural, personal, and religious diversity. The biblical story of Christmas concludes with the magi going home by another road. The inclusion in the gospel story of these wise men from another land and another faith speaks to us of God's inclusive perspective, a perspective that allows for different roads, that isn't threatened by different ideas.

We conclude our affirmation of Celtic spiritual guides with George MacLeod (1895–1991), whose incarnational vision led him to restore the monastic community on the sacred island of Iona. For MacLeod, the secular was chockfull of Divinity. We can experience God every moment, he believed, "for the simple reason that God is life: not religious life or church life but the whole [of] life. . . . God is the Life of life."[35] Creation is "resplendent" with Divinity, the eternal seeps through the physical world, so that all Creation is filled with God's glory.[36] Our social responsibility is grounded in the sacredness of all life, MacLeod taught, and in today's world that includes everything from economics and immigration to health care and housing. "The secular is the realm of God's activity and . . . He is in and through all things."[37]

As the magi teach us, there are many roads to spirituality and salvation. Our own lives may involve unexpected detours: job loss, health crises, relational changes, and encounters with persons of other faiths and cultures. Changes related to the aging process force us to find a new course and alter our personal vision in order to creatively respond to new life situations. Political upheaval may drive us from complacency to prophetic challenge. The road that lies ahead of each of us will be filled with holy surprises that ask us to expand our understanding of ourselves, of others, and of God.

Christmas treasures otherness: marginalized shepherds, mystical angels, nocturnal revelations, holiness in a humble family, and enlightenment from practitioners of other faiths. The true Light enlightens all persons and illuminates every path we travel. All we need is to know that God blesses our footsteps and the pathways we travel. *And so let us pray that the Christmas journey awakens us to thin places everywhere.*

Be Thou my vision, oh Lord of my heart;
Naught be all else to me, save that Thou art.
Thou my best thought by day or by night,
Waking or sleeping, Thy presence my light.[38]

A CHRISTMAS PRACTICE

Christmas is a vision quest, inspiring us to new ways of seeing and being. The Lakota people have a tradition of crying out for a vision, and in a similar way, Celtic Christians prayed for Divine guidance and providential inspiration. Today, consider how your life might become a prayer for vision and insight, compassion and love. Look for holiness in all the "others" you encounter and silently bless each one—and if called upon, reach out to bless, welcome, and comfort the others in your life.

A CHRISTMAS PRAYER

Loving God, give me vision. Help me hear the singing of angels and the crying of children. Let my prayers take shape in loving words and healing hands. Walk with me, and help me walk with the lost and lonely, the forgotten and marginalized. Let my life be an incarnation of that little Child who is our Savior. Amen.

SOURCES

1. Carl McColman, *An Invitation to Celtic Wisdom: A Little Guide to Mystery, Spirit, and Compassion* (Charlotte, NC: Hampton Roads, 2018), p. 6.

2. David Adam, *Flame in My Heart: Saint Aidan for Today* (Harrisburg, PA: Morehouse, 1997), pp. 23–24.

3. J. Phillip Newell, *The Book of Creation: An Introduction to Celtic Spirituality* (Mahweh, NJ: Paulist Press, 1999), p. xxi.

4. Ibid., p. 40.

5. Kenneth McIntosh, *Water from an Ancient Well: Celtic Spirituality for Modern Life* (Vestal, NY: Anamchara Books, 2011), p. 17.

6. Robert Van de Weyer, *Celtic Fire* (London: Darton, Longman, and Todd, 1990), p. 79.

7. Ibid., p. 80.

8. Esther de Waal, *Every Earthly Blessing* (Harrisburg, PA: Moorehouse, 1999), p. 9.

9. Van de Weyer, p. 77.

10. de Waal, p. 5.

11. To read more about this incident, see *Brigid's Mantle: A Celtic Dialogue Between Pagan and Christian* by Lilly Weichberger and Kenneth McIntosh (Vestal, NY: Anamchara Books, 2015), pp. 97–98.

12. Phillips Brooks (1835–1893), "O Little Town of Bethlehem."

13. Quoted in Newell, p. 8.

14. Quoted in Philip Sheldrake, *Living Between Two Worlds* (London: Dartman, Longman & Todd, 1995), p. 76.

15. Adam, p. 22.

16. Van de Weyer, pp. 92–93.

17. Quoted in Van de Weyer, p. 96.

18. Ibid., p. 93.

19. Ibid., pp. 20–21.

20. Quoted in McColman, p. 92.

21. Quoted in Van de Weyer, p. 80.

22. A more extended discussion of Patrick's life is found in McColman, pp. 77–87.

23. Quoted in de Waal, pp. 104.

24. Van de Weyer, p. 76.

25. Quoted with permission in Bruce Epperly, *The Work of Christmas: The Twelve Days of Christmas with Howard Thurman* (Vestal, NY: Anamchara Books, 2017), p. 44

26. Adam, pp. 106, 109.

27. Ibid., p. 144.

28. Quoted in Van de Weyer, p. 92; the "Song of Amergin" is an ancient poem thought to have been orally transmitted from some distant time before the Roman invasion. According to legend, it is the first poem of the British Isles and was created when Amergin, a prehistoric bard, first set foot on what is today Ireland.

29. For a more extended discussion of Brendan, see Carl McColman's *An Invitation to Celtic Wisdom*, pp. 105–115. The complete account of Brendan's voyage, based on the ancient accounts, can be found in *Celtic Miracles and Wonders: Tales from the Ancient Saints* (Vestal, NY: Anamchara Books, 2015), pp. 81–103.

30. Quoted in McIntosh, pp. 55.

31. Quoted in de Waal, p. xxi.

32. Quoted in J. Philip Newell, *Listening for the Heart of God: A Celtic Spirituality* (Mahweh, NJ: Paulist, 1997), p. 63.

33. Ibid., 64.

34. Quoted in de Waal, p. 9.

35. Quoted in Newell, *Listening to the Heartbeat of God*, p. 76.

36. Ibid., p. 86.

37. Ibid., p. 90.

38. Ancient Celtic hymn, said to have been written by Dallán Forgaill in the sixth century.

To find out more about Celtic spirituality, you might also read these books from Anamchara Books:

- *Celtic Christianity: Deep Roots for a Modern Faith* by Ray Simpson
- *A Celtic Book of Days: Ancient Wisdom for Each Day of the Year from the Celtic Followers of Christ* by Ray Simpson
- *Celtic Nature Prayers: Prayers from an Ancient Well* by Kenneth McIntosh

THE WORK OF CHRISTMAS
The 12 Days of Christmas with Howard Thurman

This book is a celebration of the twelve days of Christmas, offering us a chance to dwell on the meaning of the season in dialogue with the wisdom of one of America's greatest mystics and activists, Howard Thurman.

During the twelve days of Christmas, our goal is to experience God's light, despite the temptation to close our hearts in a world too often characterized by racism, sexism, polarization, nationalism, and exclusion. This season asks us instead to open our hearts and our lives, so that throughout the year ahead,

we may be light-bearers, carrying the message of Divine justice and hope, making it come alive even in the darkest corners of the world. This is the year-round work of Christmas!

Paperback Price: $10.99

Kindle Price: $5.99

I WONDER AS I WANDER
The 12 Days of Christmas with Madeleine L'Engle

How can we recover the radical meaning of the Christmas season? Using the thoughts and words of Madeleine L'Engle, this books offers you a guide through the hectic Christmas season. In the twelve days of Christmas, bookended by Christmas Eve and the Feast of Epiphany, you will experience anew the awe and wonder of the Incarnation. As you both wonder and wander, the questions and images in this book will open your heart to the radical message of Christmas. Like the Magi, you too can follow a star, seeking wisdom in everyday life, while contemplating the cosmic forces within which we live and move and have our being.

Paperback Price: $10.99

Kindle Price: $5.99

BECOME FIRE!

Guideposts for Interspiritual Pilgrims

In the spirit of God's call to creative transformation, Bruce Epperly invites you to join him on a holy adventure in spiritual growth, inspired by the evolving wisdom of Christianity and the world's great spiritual traditions, innovative global spiritual practices, and emerging visions of reality. Epperly explores the many resources of Christian spirituality in dialogue with the spiritual practices of the world's great wisdom traditions, describing the gifts other spiritual paths contribute to the pathway of Jesus; at the same time, he uses the lens of the spiritual practices Jesus has inspired throughout Christian history to examine these spiritual paths.

Paperback Price: $24.95

Kindle Price: $8.99

SANTA CLAUS
Saint, Shaman, & Symbol

If you don't believe in Santa, you might want to reconsider. The familiar fellow dressed in red has been around a lot longer than the malls' Santa, longer than Rudolph, longer even than "The Night Before Christmas." His earliest and most ancient forms brought hope and cheer to generation after generation of humankind—and he still has a message for us today. In the midst of the materialism of the modern holiday, Santa offers us a bridge between the physical, secular world and the spiritual, sacred realm. Discover his history and evolution, from Ice Age shaman to medieval saint to modern-day icon. Get to know Santa—and believe all over again.

Paperback Price: $12.95

Kindle Price: $5.99

BRUCE EPPERLY is pastor of South Congregational Church, Centerville, Massachusetts, and a professor in theology and spirituality at Wesley Theological Seminary, Washington, DC. He is also the author of more than forty-five books on theology, spirituality, healing, ministry, and scripture, including *The Mystic in You: Discovering a God-Filled World*, *Become Fire!: Guideposts for Interspiritual Pilgrims*, *The Work of Christmas: The 12 Days of Christmas with Howard Thurman,* and *I Wonder as I Wander: The 12 Days of Christmas with Madeleine L'Engle.*. He lives on Cape Cod, where he is an avid beach walker, grandparent, husband, father, and advocate for environmental care.

AnamcharaBooks.com

www.ingramcontent.com/pod-product-compliance
Lightning Source LLC
Chambersburg PA
CBHW060529080526
44586CB00012B/675